SQUAREKNITS
A New Approach to
GRANNY SQUARES

Clouds (page 56), to fit an average ten-year-old

SQUAREKNITS
A New Approach to
GRANNY SQUARES

VAL GUILFORD

Photography by Robert McCree

Kangaroo Press

This book is dedicated to the memories of
my father, my sister, and Pop, my father-in-law

Acknowledgments
I would like to thank everyone who has helped and
supported me throughout my endeavours—my models,
my mother and especially Roger my husband, Ron van
Hamelsveld, who helped with the word processing and
computer graphics, and Isabel who, along with Angelie,
helped me with the knitting; also, Colgate Palmolive Ltd
and Thorobred Yarns.

© Val Guilford 1992

First published in 1992 by Kangaroo Press Pty Ltd
3 Whitehall Road (P.O. Box 75) Kenthurst 2156
Typeset by G.T. Setters Pty Limited
Printed in Hong Kong by Colorcraft Ltd.

ISBN 0 86417 440 3

Contents

Foreword

When I first started to teach this new concept of knitting, my only thought was to give to young and inexperienced knitters a pattern that was simple, and would enable them to knit a garment in a relatively short time.

The concept behind squareknits has proved acceptable to many knitters, however, and now the experienced as well use it in some of their work. It has proven to be a successful addition to basic knitting.

Your imagination is the only limit, and I wish you all 'happy knitting'.

Val Guilford

Abbreviations

st	stitch
sts	stitches
k	knit
rep	repeat
beg	beginning
fol	following
cont	continue
meas	measures
gt st	garter st
M	main colour
con A B C	contrast; as colours are added they become A, B, C, etc.
tog	together
psso	pass slip stitch over
sl 1	slip one
m 1	make one, by putting the wool over the needle and knitting as a stitch in the next row

inc	increase; the increasing is worked by knitting into the front and the back of the first stitch (unless I have stated otherwise), and only at the **beginning of each row**, until you have the required number of stitches for your garment
dec	decrease; the decreasing is knit 1, knit 2 together, only at the **beginning of each row**, unless otherwise stated. Continue knitting until you have 3 stitches on your needle, slip 1 st, knit 2 tog, pass slip stitch over, fasten off
HWR	halfway row
st st	stocking stitch; right side row is knit, wrong side row going back is purl
tbl	through back of loop

Conversion tables

Needles

14	2 mm	5	5.5 mm
12	2.25 mm	4	6 mm
11	3 mm	3	6.5 mm
10	3.25 mm	2	7 mm
9	3.75 mm	1	7.5 mm
8	4 mm	0	8 mm
7	4.5 mm	00	9 mm
6	5 mm	000	10 mm

Measurements

inches	mm	inches	mm
18	45	36	90
20	50	38	95
22	55	40	100
24	60	42	105
26	65	44	110
28	70	46	115
30	75	48	120
32	80	50	125
34	85	52	130

Calculating measurements

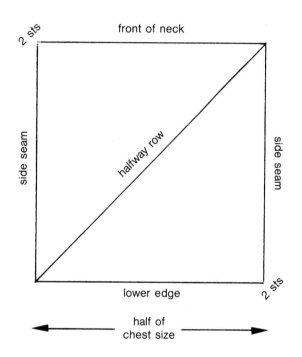

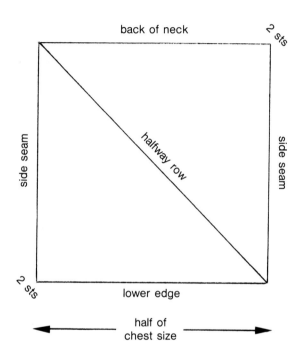

If the garment is intended for a person with an 85 cm (34″) chest measurement, keep knitting the increase until the lower edge of the square measures half the chest measurement, i.e. 43 cm (17″).

Squares for a garment based on a 4-square front or back (see Peach Parfait, page 25) would only need to be half this measurement, i.e. in this example the lower edge of the square would be 21.5 cm (8½″).

Basic granny square pattern

Materials   *Illustrated on page 11*
50 g 8-ply wool
5 mm needles

Cast on 2 sts
Knit these 2 sts.
Increases (inc) start now.
At the **beginning of every row** inc until you have 30 sts
(approx 10 cm).
Knit one row without inc. This is the middle row of your
square and will be known throughout the patterns as the
halfway row (HWR).
Now decrease **at the beginning of every row** until you have
3 sts left.
Slip 1 st st, knit 2 together, pass slip stitch over (sl 1, k2 tog,
psso). Fasten off.

You have now learnt how to knit the **basic square**. This is
all that is necessary to knit any of the basic square patterns.
As you go through the book you will find how to knit
garments for any member of your family. By knitting the
basic rectangle you will able to knit the garments longer.
There is also a **basic batwing** which can make your garment
very stylish.

You have wool, needles and the patterns, so away you go
and knit yourself a garment without tears, remembering that
I had to start off without this book. (And, yes, there were
tears. . .)

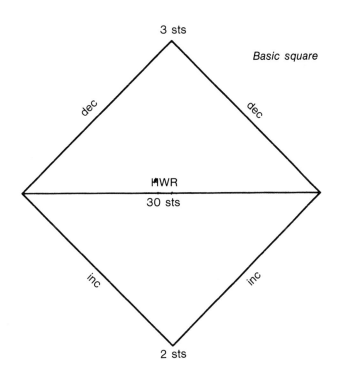

3 sts

Basic square

dec   dec

HWR
30 sts

inc   inc

2 sts

9

Basic batwing pattern

Materials
50 g 8-ply wool
5 mm needles

The basic batwing is used for making a loose sleeve. It is very simple to knit. It starts off with the basic square inc, and ends with the basic square dec. Knit yourself this small sample first.

The seam is on the shoulder instead of under the arm. I enjoy wearing this sleeve on my garments.

Cast on 2 sts; knitting the basic inc, knit until you have 30 sts. Mark one side of your work with a coloured thread. Continue knitting basic inc on the side with the coloured thread. At the same time, when you start the next row on the unmarked side, knit the basic dec (which is knit 1, knit 2 tog). You will have 31 sts on your needle on the inc row; when you knit the dec row you will have 30 sts.
Continue this way until you have knitted 10 rows.
Knit a halfway row.
You now will knit the other way, dec on the side with the coloured thread and inc on the other side. The bit like a fish's mouth is the wrist edge.
Continue knitting this way, 30 sts on the dec row and 31 sts on the inc row, for 10 rows. Then, knitting the basic square dec pattern, continue until you have 3 sts left, sl 1, k2 tog, psso.
Fasten off.

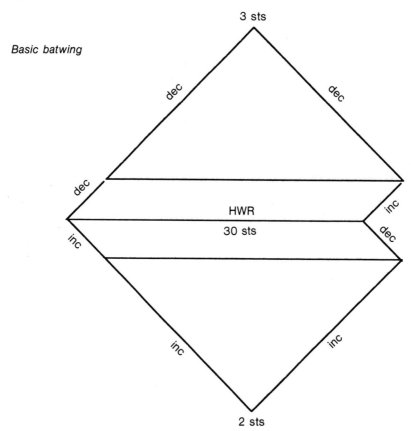

Basic batwing

3 sts

dec dec

dec inc

HWR
30 sts

inc dec

inc inc

2 sts

10

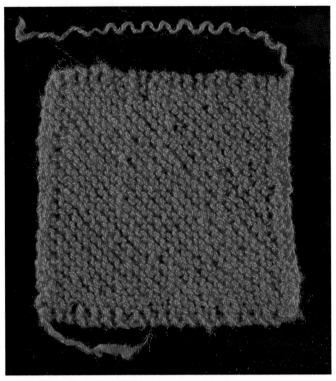

Example of the basic granny square (page 9)

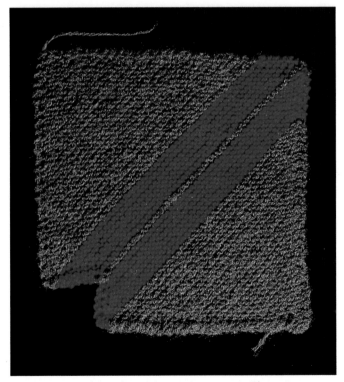

Example of the basic batwing (previous page). The stripes emphasise the special increase and decrease areas, and the halfway row

Example of the basic rectangle (page 13). The stripes indicate the position of the two 'halfway rows'

Basic rectangle pattern

Materials
50 g 8-ply wool
5 mm needles

Illustrated on page 11

The basic rectangle pattern is used for knitting the fronts of cardigans and coats; it can also be used for knitting the front of a jumper.

Knit the basic square pattern until you have 40 sts on your needle. Mark one side with a coloured thread.

Knit the basic inc as before on the side with the coloured thread and on the other side knit the basic dec. On the inc side you will have 41 sts; on the dec side you will have 40 sts.

Instructions for working out measurements are in the front of the book.

For this sample, knit the 40-41 sts for 10 rows, knit the halfway row, then knit the basic dec.

Fasten off.

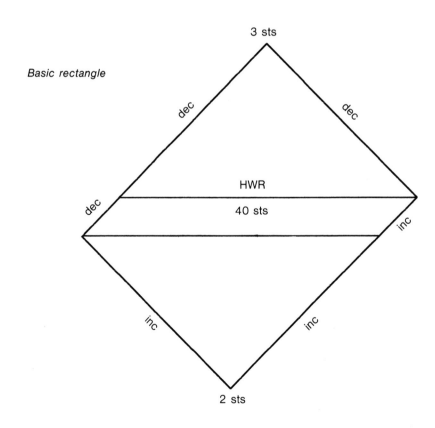

Basic rectangle

3 sts

dec   dec

HWR

40 sts

dec   inc

inc   inc

2 sts

The patterns

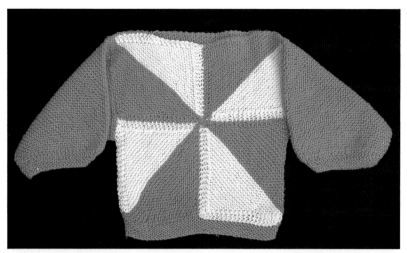

Windmill jumper (page 17). The windmill is just one way of arranging this pattern

Penny models the Little Tank Top (page 16) striped in lilac and white

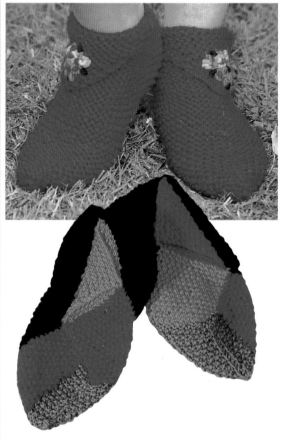

Jester slippers, livened up with flowers and knitted in harlequin colours (page 16)

Penny modelling Love-in-the-mist in soft blue and white (page 16). The collar is trimmed with a lover's knot knitted like a tie bow (page 60)

Love-in-the-mist knitted in cream and aqua with the alternative soft collar (page 17)

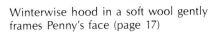

Winterwise hood in a soft wool gently frames Penny's face (page 17)

Jester slippers

Materials   *Illustrated on page 14*
150 g of either 8-ply or 14-ply wool
5 mm needles
wide-eyed darning needle
50 cm hat elastic (optional)

This pattern is for a 23 cm foot.
Knit 2 alike.
Knit basic granny square pattern inc. If using 8-ply wool, work until you have 60 sts, and if using 14-ply wool work until you have 46 sts.
Knit the halfway row then, knitting the basic pattern, dec until 5 sts remain.
Break off the wool, leaving enough thread to sew up the first slipper.
Thread the darning needle and run it through the remaining 5 sts, gathering them firmly. Do not break thread. Sew the slipper along the foot, and up the back of the heel, making sure to leave enough room for your foot to slide through with comfort. Finish by securing the thread neatly, and cut off.
You may like to thread some hat elastic around the ankles to make the slippers feel more secure, although this is not essential.
Multicoloured jester slippers are a good way of using up oddments of yarn.

Little tank top

Materials   *Illustrated on page 14*
200 g 8-, 12- or 14-ply wool for main colour (M)
50 g 8-, 12- or 14-ply wool for contrast (con A)
5 mm needles

Front
Knit the basic square with M until you have 20 sts.
Join in con A, knitting basic pattern for 2 rows.
Change to M, knit 2 rows.
Change to con A, knit 2 rows.
Cont this way until you have 30 sts.
Change back to M, knit until you have 40 sts. Knit stripes again in con A and M, alternately, until 50 sts are on the needle.
Knit in M to 60 sts.
Change to con A, knit 2 rows.
Knit 2 rows with M (64 sts).
Next row is the halfway row.

Knit 2 rows with con A. This garment has 3 halfway rows so the shoulder corner has a good point on it.
Continuing with basic square dec; keeping stripes even knit until you have 20 sts.
Finish the basic square dec, knitting only in M. Fasten off.

Back
The back can be striped like the front, or plain. Either way knit the basic square pattern.

Back and front bands
Knit the bands before you sew the seams.
Pick up 40 sts along the lower edge of each piece. (Knit the bands separately, making a tidy seam. This will fit better than knitting the band all in one.)
Knit each 40 sts for 12 rows.
Cast off loosely, and sew up seams.

Love-in-the-mist jumper

Materials   *Illustrated on page 15*
200 g 8-ply wool for main colour M
50 g 8-ply wool for con A
5 mm needles
darning needle

Back and sleeves (3 alike)
Knit the basic square in M to 70 sts.
Knit the halfway row.
Knit the basic square dec.
Fasten off.

Front
Knit basic square in M to 8 sts.
Knit 2 rows in con A.
Continue alternating M with con A, 2 rows of each, without breaking off wool, until you have 72 sts.
Knit the halfway row and continue knitting in stripes. Finish the basic square dec pattern.

Sleeve bands (2 alike)
In con A, pick up and knit 36 sts across the lower edge of the square.
Knit 8 to 10 rows in either gt st or k1, p1 rib.
Cast off.

Bands for front and back
Pick up 60 sts and once again knit in either gt st or k1, p1 rib for 8 to 10 rows.
Cast off loosely.

Collar (sewn on)
Cast on 70 sts in con A.
K 2 rows.
Next row inc in every 5th st (84 sts).
K 3 rows.
Next row inc in every 5th st (100 sts).
K 3 rows.
Knit another row inc in every 5th st (120 sts).
Knit one row and cast off. You should have 12 rows altogether. Sew to neckline.
You may like to knit a deeper collar. If you do, keep increasing as before, otherwise the collar will not sit neatly.

Soft collar
This is another collar that you might like to try—it is very comfortable to wear and I find that it sits well on several of the garments. Where the first collar was sewn on, this one you begin by picking up stitches.
Sew together one shoulder of the jumper, and pick up sts evenly around the neck. The number of sts will vary with the size of your garment. The neckband on page 57 may be helpful here.
After you have picked up the sts knit in k1, p1 rib for 6 rows.
7th row, inc into every k st.
8th row, inc into every k st.
You now have a k2, p2 rib.
Knit in k2, p2 rib until you have worked 12 rows for a child and 16 to 18 rows for an adult.
Cast off.

Windmill jumper

Materials   *Illustrated on page 14*
200 g 8-ply wool for main colour
50 g 8-ply wool for con A
5 mm needles

Front (4 alike)
With M knit the basic square to 40 sts.
Change to con A and knit the halfway row.
With con A finish knitting the basic square dec.

Back
With M knit the basic square to 75 sts.
Knit the halfway row.
Knit the basic square dec.

Sleeves (4 alike)
With M knit the basic square pattern to 50 sts.
Knit the halfway row.
Knit the basic square dec.

Cuffs
Knitting with M, pick up 56 sts.
Knit 1 row, dec every 7th st by knitting 7th and 8th sts tog, (49 sts).
Next row, dec every 5th st by knitting 5th and 6th sts tog, (42 sts).
Knit one row.
Cast off.

Bands
For the back and front knit the same bands as for Love-in-the-mist (previous pattern).

Winterwise hood

Materials   *Illustrated on page 15*
300 g very soft wool
6 or 7 mm needles

Hood
Knit the basic square pattern to 90 sts.
This is a good point to check the fit around the wearer's head. To do this take the cast-on point, fold up to the tip of the needle and stretch a little. If it is half the head measurement carry on knitting; if it is too small now is the time to inc the number of sts.
Knit the halfway row.
Knit the basic square pattern dec. Fasten off.

Yoke
Pick up 85 sts from the inc edge of the square you have just knitted, and knit 3 rows. (If you have made your square bigger, you will be picking up more sts.)
Knit 3 rows.
Next row, inc into every 5th st (102 sts).
Knit 3 rows.
Next row, inc into every 6th st (119 sts).
Knit 3 rows.
Next row, inc into every 6th st (139 sts).
Knit 5 rows.
Next row, inc into every 6th st (162 sts).
Knit 5 rows.
Next row, inc into every 6th st (189 sts).
Knit 1 row. Cast off.
Sew up the side seam.

I advise you to make this hood in a very soft wool. It will be worn around the face. Some harder wools can be very irritating on the face, even aggravating allergies.

Fuchsia jumper demonstrates a variety of stripe patterns. The
detail picture shows the crossed-over neck tie (page 20)

Penny's Hyacinth jumper, in two-toned blue, is trimmed around the neck and down the front with a simple knitted frill (page 21)

Fuchsia jumper

Illustrated on page 18

Materials
250 g 8-ply wool, M
100 g 8-ply wool, con A
5 mm needles

Front

Knit the basic pattern with M to 20 sts.
Change to con A and knit 4 rows (24 sts).
Knit 12 rows with M (36 sts).
*Now knit the fine stripes:
    2 rows in con A (38 sts)
    2 rows in M (40 sts)
    2 rows in con A (42 sts)
    2 rows in M (44 sts)
    2 rows in con A (46 sts)*
The last 10 rows are referred to throughout this pattern as 'fine stripes, 2 rows of each colour'.*
Knit 12 rows in M (58 sts).
Knit from * to * (68 sts).
Knit 12 rows in M (80 sts).
With con A knit the halfway row (80 sts).

Now we divide the 80 sts; knitting the basic dec pattern knit 40 sts separately.
With con A knit 1 row.
Change to M and knit 12 rows (27 sts).
Knit from * to * (17 sts).
Knit 12 rows in M (5 sts).
Change to con A and finish the basic pattern dec.
Fasten off.

On the remaining 40 sts, starting in the centre of the work knit 1 row in con A.
Start knitting the basic dec pattern (39 sts).

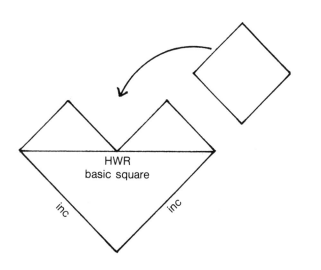

HWR
basic square
inc
inc

Knit 6 rows in M (33 sts).
Knit 4 rows in con A (29 sts).
Knit 6 rows in M (23 sts).
Knit 4 rows in con A (19 sts).
Knit 6 rows in M ·(13 sts).
Knit 4 rows in con A (9 sts).
Finish the basic pattern in M. Fasten off.

Insert

Knit the basic pattern in fine stripes, starting with M.
Knit to 42 sts.
Knit the halfway row.
Working in fine stripes, dec until you have 12 sts.
Finish knitting basic pattern in con A.
Fasten off.

Back

Knit the basic pattern until you have 80 sts.
Knit the halfway row, then finish knitting the basic pattern.
Fasten off.

Sleeve one

Knit the basic pattern in fine stripes to 68 sts. You should end in con A.
Change to M and knit to 76 sts.
Knit the halfway row.
Finish the basic dec pattern, knitting with M.

Sleeve two

Knit the basic pattern in M to 58 sts.
Change to con A, knit 4 rows (62 sts).
Continue knitting the pattern in M to 76 sts.
Knit the halfway row.
Finish the basic pattern dec.
Fasten off.

Sleeve bands

Pick up 39 sts and knit 14 rows in con A.

Back and front bands

Follow Love-in-the-mist (page 16).

Neck tie

Knit the basic pattern with con A to 24 sts.
Next row, k2 tog along the row (12 sts).
K2, k2 tog, k2 tog, k2 tog, k2 tog, k2 (8 sts).
On these 8 sts knit until your work measures the same as the neck edge. Getting this measurement is easier if you have sewn the shoulders together.
Allow 4 ridges (8 rows) on both sides.
Next row, k2 sts, inc into the next 4 sts, k2 (12 sts).
Next row, inc into every st (24 sts).
Finish knitting the basic square dec. Fasten off.
Sew around the neck edge and sew a dome or press-stud on the tie as a fastener.

Hyacinth jumper

Materials   *Illustrated on page 19*
250 g 8-ply wool for M
50 g 8-ply wool for con A
5 mm needles

Back and sleeves (alike)
These three pieces are all knitted in M.

Knit basic square pattern inc to 80 sts.
Knit the halfway row.
Knit the basic square dec.
Fasten off.

Front
The front is knitted with an insert like the previous pattern, Fuchsia. If you would like to change the stripe sequence please do so. (You might wish to add another colour.) There are no hard and fast rules with knitting this way—the only thing is, make sure you have enough wool.

Knit the basic square pattern with M until you have 22 sts.
Change to con A, knit 6 rows (28 sts).
With M knit 6 rows (34 sts).
Change to con A, knit 6 rows (40 sts).
With M knit 6 rows (46 sts).
With con A knit 6 rows (52 sts).
With M knit 12 rows (64 sts).

Starting with con A, knit the fine stripes, 2 rows of each colour, until you have 78 sts.
Knit 1 row in M (79 sts).
Knit the halfway row. Now divide the work (40 sts on one side, 39 on the other).

Knit the two sides separately. In the basic square dec in the first half until you have 28 sts on your needle.
Knit the fine stripes, starting with con A, until you have 14 sts.
Change to M, knit 6 rows (8 sts).
With con A finish knitting the basic square dec pattern.
Knit the other half the same way, starting in the middle and dec straight away so that both sides are even.

Insert
Knitting the basic square pattern, start with con A and knit until you have 6 sts.
Change to M. Knit fine stripes with M and con A until you have 36 sts. The last row should be M (but do not worry if it isn't).
Change to con A and knit the halfway row.
Knitting the basic dec pattern, work with con A and knit 7 rows.

Change to M, knit 6 rows.
With con A knit 4 rows.
With M knit 4 rows.
With con A knit 4 rows.
Knitting this way finish the basic dec.
Fasten off.

Bands
Knit the bands from the pattern Love-in-the-mist for the front, the back and the sleeves.

Frill
Allow yourself plenty of time to knit this as it is quite time consuming.

Cast on 160 sts, knit 1 row.
Next row, inc into every st (320 sts).
Cast off.
Knit another frill, casting on 100 sts and inc to 200 sts.
Cast off.

Sewing up
Sew the insert to match the stripes, if possible.
Sew the shoulders for 7 or 8 cm.
Sew sleeves in, then sew up all the side seams.

The 320 sts frill is sewn around the neck and the 200 sts frill is sewn up the front along the edge of the insert.

This frill is a good trim to put on other garments, and apart from the time it takes is easy to knit.

The Comet pattern (page 24) shown here before the addition of the sleeves

Peach Parfait, a very useful sleeveless V-necked top, is modelled by Sarah (page 25)

Penny's Favourite (modelled by Penny) is described on page 25

Comet jumper

Illustrated on page 22

Materials
200 g 8-ply wool for M
50 g 8-ply wool for con A
5 mm needles

Sleeves (4 alike)
*Knit the basic pattern, inc in M until you have 41 sts.
Change to con A, knit 2 rows (43 sts).
With M knit 2 rows (45 sts).
Change to con A and knit the halfway row.
Still with con A, start the basic dec and knit 7 rows (38 sts)*.
Change to M and finish the square.

Front (3 squares alike)
Knit the basic pattern inc in M, following basic sleeve pattern * to *.
With M, knitting the basic dec, now knit 8 rows (30 sts).
Divide the sts (15 sts).
Basic dec then knit (12 sts). Put the other 15 sts onto a holder.
Turn, knit to the end of the row without any shaping.
Knitting like this, with only 1 dec on the outside edge, finish the square.
Knitting with con A on the remaining sts, knit the basic square dec **but only on the outside edge**, opposite to the piece you have just knitted.
Finish the square.

Fourth square
Knit the basic pattern * to *, then 2 rows in M.
With con A knit 2 rows.
With M knit 2 rows, then 2 rows with con A. Divide sts and finish off like the other 3 squares.

Back
Knit 4 squares as for the front. When you divide the sts, where you knitted with M knit con A for the back, and where you knitted with con A, knit with M.

Bands
Pick up 60 sts, knitting separately for back and front. Knit in gt st or rib, 8 to 10 rows. Cast off.

Sew all pieces together. If you wish you can knit a collar, otherwise sew together, using the Plunket shoulder (page 60, Miscellany).

Penny's Favourite jumper

Illustrated on page 23

Materials
200 g 8-ply wool for M
100 g 8-ply wool for con A
100 g 8-ply wool for con B
5 mm needles

Front and back (alike)
8 squares in all.

Using M wool, cast on 2 sts, and knit basic square pattern until you have 24 sts.
Change to con A. Knitting basic pattern, knit 12 rows (36 sts).
Change to con B, knit 4 rows (40 sts).
Knit the next 2 rows without inc. These are the halfway rows. (Two rows are needed here so that the colours in the pattern are equal.)
Continue with the basic square pattern dec, knitting with con B until you have 36 sts.
Change to con A, knit 12 rows (24 sts).
Change to M and finish knitting the basic square dec.
Fasten off.

Sleeves (2 alike)
The sleeves are short, but you can make them longer by knitting 4 extra squares. For long sleeves knit the band from Love-in-the-mist (page 16).
Knit 4 basic squares, knitting from 2 sts to 40 sts.
Knit the halfway row.
Finish off the basic square dec.

Bands
Knit the bands as for the jumper Love-in-the-mist, with 60 sts to 65 sts for 10 to 12 rows.
Cast off.

Collar
Knitting with the main colour, knit 6 basic squares inc to 16 sts, leaving them all on the needle. Then on all the 96 sts knit for 3 or 4 rows before casting off. The collar is sewn onto the neck as you sew your garment up.

Peach Parfait jumper

Materials   *Illustrated on page 22*

200 g 8-ply wool for M
50 g 8-ply wool for con A
5 mm needles

Back
Knit 4 basic squares from 2 sts to 40 sts.
Knit the halfway row, then knit the basic square dec, 40 sts to 3 sts, sl 1, k2 tog, psso.
Fasten off.

If you want to knit this to a different size, inc until the bottom edge of the square equals half the front measurement (larger or smaller). When you come to the neckband the number of sts will differ from the pattern, but this is not a problem—it is easy to work out.

Front
Knit 2 basic squares to 40 sts.
Knit the halfway row, then knit the basic square dec.
Fasten off.

Knit the 2 neck squares as follows:
Knit the basic square to 40 sts.
Knit the halfway row.
Knit the basic dec until you have 30 sts on your needle.
Put these sts on a stitch holder.

Making up
Sew the 4 squares together for the back.
Sew the 4 squares together for the front, leaving the neck squares on the stitch holders.
Sew one side seam, but only as far as the first square.

Waistband
Pick up and knit in garter st 120 sts, separately for front and back.
Next row knit.
Change to k1, p1 rib and knit in rib for 11 rows.
You may knit 2 rows M, 2 rows A, if you wish, but finish with the main colour. Cast off in rib.

Neckband
Sew one shoulder seam together.
With the right side of your work facing, pick up and knit 30 sts from one stitch holder.
Pick up a stitch between the 2 squares at the front for the centre stitch of the V neckline. It is a good idea to mark this st with a bright coloured wool.
Pick up the next 30 sts from the other stitch holder, then along the back of the neck pick up another 30 sts (91 sts).

Turn work around and knit in k1, p1 rib for 58 sts, k2 tog, p1 (this is the centre st), k2 tog. Knitting in rib finish the row. Next row, rib 27 sts, p2 tog, k1, p2 tog, rib to the end of row. Continue knitting this way, dec either side of the centre st for 4 rows. Cast off in rib. On the cast-off row still work the dec.
Fasten off.

Buttons
Knit 4 basic squares to 6 sts.
Knit the halfway row, then finish with the basic dec.
Leave a thread long enough to sew a running st around the square to draw it into a circle. (This is done the same way as the flower centre on page 63).
Sew the buttons onto the garment.

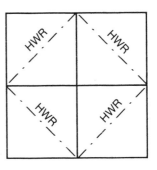

V neck

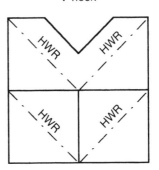

Two versions of the Basic Baby's Garment (page 28): left, with frogged fastenings for a larger baby, and below, pink and pretty for a little girl, with tiny Jester slippers to match

A warm and snuggly sleeping bag for a baby (page 28)

The Jade and Black Fair Isle jumper looks far more difficult than it is (page 29)

Basic baby's garment

Materials   *Illustrated on page 26*
200 g 8-ply or 4-ply wool
5 mm or 3.25 mm needles

Neither this garment, nor any of the others in this book, have to be knitted with 8-ply wool, although all the photographed examples are in 8-ply. I have knitted the 8-ply with 5 mm needles, but for 4-ply I would have used 3.25 mm needles, and so on. The table on page 60 tells you what needles to use with each ply.

Back
Cast on 2 sts and knit the basic square inc until you have 50 sts.
Knit the halfway row.
Knit the basic square pattern dec to the end, fasten off.

Fronts (knit two)
Cast on 2 sts and knit the basic square inc until you have 26 sts. Now knit the basic rectangle on these 26 sts until your work measures the same as the back seam.
Make the buttonholes, **on one rectangle only**, on the dec side, about 3 cm apart. Knit the dec, (m1, k2 tog), buttonhole, then knit to end.
Knit a halfway row, then knit the basic square dec until you have 17 sts left. Leave these sts on a spare needle or stitch holder for the neckband.

Sleeves
Cast on 2 sts and knit the basic square inc to 43 sts.
Knit the halfway row.
Knit the basic square dec. Fasten off.

Bands for the sleeves
Pick up 26 sts (I find it's best to do this on the inc edge) and knit in k1, p1 rib for 6 rows, casting off on the 7th row.

Neckband
Sew the shoulders tog, then knit 17 sts off the spare needle, 15 sts across the back of the neck, then the other 17 sts (49 sts). Knit 6 rows. Cast off.

The photographs show two versions of this pattern, and I know that you will soon work out some favourites of your own. The little pink garment has a small pair of bootees with it, and can be a lovely gift for a new baby. It has no bands, but a crocheted thread for the wrists instead, and is trimmed with the frill from Hyacinth, page 21 (with fewer sts to fit). This pattern suits any shade of wool.

Baby's sleeping bag/coat/ dressing gown

Materials   *Illustrated on page 27*
400 g of double knitting wool
51 cm zip
4 mm needles

Back
Cast on 3 sts.
Knit 1 row.
K1, m1, knit to end.
Continue these 2 rows to 106 sts. Mark with coloured wool here.
K1, m1, knit to end.
K1, k2 tog, knit to end.
Knit this way until the work measures 52 cm.
K1, k2 tog, knit to end.
Continue until you have 3 sts; finish the basic square dec. Fasten off.

Front (make 2)
Cast on 3 sts.
Knit 1 row.
K1, m1, knit to end.
Continue to 52 sts.
K1, m1, knit to end.
K1, k2 tog, knit to end.
Knit this way until work measures 52 cm.
K1, k2 tog, knit to end.
Knit the basic square dec. Fasten off.

Sleeves and hat (make 4)
Cast on 3 sts, knit basic square pattern to 60 sts.
Knit the halfway row.
Knit the basic square dec. Fasten off.

Making up
Sew the shoulders for 12 cm. Sew in sleeves (one square each). Then sew the lower edge (if making a sleeping bag) and about 9 cm at the lower middle front seam. (This is the seam below the zip.)
Sew underarm and side seams.
Sew two squares tog for the back seam of the hat, and sew the lower edge to the neck edge. Sew the crown seam and turn 5 cm back at each side of the hat to make a facing. Sew facing down and add a cord. I used a crochet cord because it is soft, and will stay tied up.
Add a tassel to each end of the cord.
Last of all sew in a zip, making sure to sew close to the zip so that knitting will not catch when the zip is opened or closed.
Press garment lightly.

Jade and Black Fair Isle jumper

Materials　　　　　　　　*Illustrated on page 27*
200 g 8-ply for M
100 g 8-ply for con A
5 mm needles

Front
Knit the basic pattern in M to 20 sts.
With con A knit 2 rows (22 sts).
Remember the pattern inc as you go.
Knit 6 rows in M.
Next 2 rows, with M knit the inc, then (k1 M, k1 con A) to end. On the row back make sure to knit M over M, and con A over con A.
Knit 6 rows in M.
Knit 2 rows (k2 M, k2 con A).
Knit 6 rows in M.
Knit 2 rows in con A.
Knit 6 rows in M.
The next 2 rows (k1 M, k1 con A) to end.
Knit 6 rows in M.
Knit 2 rows con A, then 6 rows in M.
Next 2 rows (k2 M, k2 con A) to end.
Knit 6 rows in M.
Knit 2 rows in con A.
Knit 6 rows in M.
Knit 2 rows (k1 M, k1 con A).
Knit 2 rows in M (88 sts).
Now **knit the halfway row twice** in M. Knit 2 more rows in M (6 rows in M altogether).

Now knit the basic dec.
*Knit 2 rows (k2 M, k2 con A).
Knit 2 rows (k4 M, k2 con A, k2 M). Finish with k4 in M.
Knit 2 rows (k8 M, k2 con A)*.
Keep 4 sts in M at the beg of all dec rows.
Knit 6 rows M.
Knit 2 rows (k1 M, k1 con A).
Knit 6 rows in M.
(Are you remembering the pattern dec?)

The next 6 rows are the zig-zag:
Knit the first 2 rows, dec over 4 sts in M, (k1 con A, k6 M). Carry wool loosely across the back, (k2 con A, k6 M, k2 con A), knit this way to end of row.
Next 2 rows dec over 4 sts in M, (k2 M, k2 con A) to end of row.
Next 2 rows dec over 4 sts in M, (k2 con A, k6 M, k2 con A) to end of row. Make sure you have k4 sts in M at the end. (This makes the top of the zig-zag, knitting con A over 2 M.)

Knit 6 rows in M.
Knit 2 rows in con A with M at each end.
Knit 6 rows in M.
Knitting with con A and M, knit 6 rows *to* of (k2 M, k2 con A).
Knit 6 rows in M.
Knit 2 rows in con A.
Knit 6 rows in M.
Knit 2 rows in con A.
Finish basic pattern in M.

Back
In M knit the basic pattern to 80 sts.
Knit the halfway row.
Finish knitting the basic pattern dec.

Neckband
You might like to use a size larger needles for the neckband.
Sew one shoulder seam together for about 7 cm. Pick up and knit 60 sts for 24 rows, cast off loosely.

Sleeve bands (knit 2)
You might like to use a size larger needles for the sleeve bands.
Sew up the other shoulder as well as the neckband. Pick up 90 sts, or more, if the armhole needs to be longer, and knit loosely for 6 rows. Cast off.
Sew side seams together.

Bands
Knit the lower bands as for Love-in-the-mist (page 16).

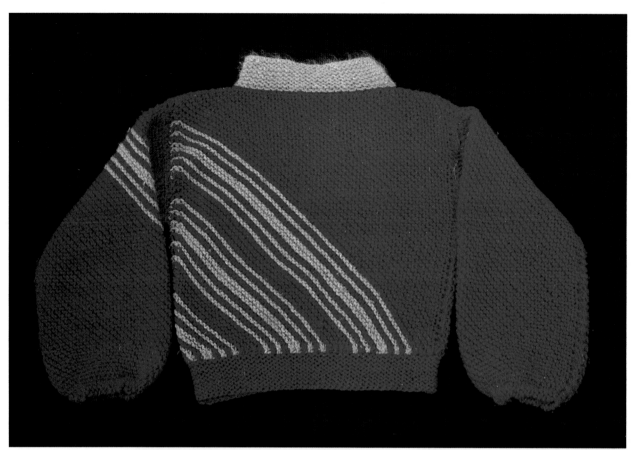

The Duet Valisa
jumper, smart with
stripes and
contrasting
neckband (page 32)

A cheerful yellow
version of Funtime
1, worn by Emma
(page 32)

Right: Sarah models
Funtime 2, another
go-anywhere, do-
anything sleeveless
top (page 33)

The pretty Domino jumper (page 33) looks difficult at first glance, but the inset picture shows how simple it really is

Duet Valisa jumper

This pattern is a standard one on which many other garments are based.

Materials   *Illustrated on page 30*
250 g 8-ply wool in M
25 g 8-ply wool in con A
5 mm needles

Back/right sleeve
Knit the basic pattern square to 80 sts.
Knit the halfway row.
Knit the basic pattern dec.

Front/left sleeve
Knit the basic pattern to 80 sts.
Knit the halfway row.
Knit basic square dec to 76 sts.
Join in con A and knit 2 rows.
With M knit 2 rows.
Continue this way, knitting 2 rows with each colour until you have knitted 8 rows.
Knit 4 rows in con A, then knit the stripes again for another 8 rows.
Front
Continue knitting the stripes, knitting the basic square dec to the end.
Sleeve
Knit the basic pattern using M to the end.

Bands
Follow the bands for back, front and sleeves from the pattern Love-in-the-mist (page 16).

Collar
Sew one shoulder seam. With con A pick up and knit 55 sts for 16 rows.
Cast off.
Sew sleeve into the other shoulder. Leave the neckband open and fold down.

Funtime jumpers 1 and 2

Materials   *Illustrated on page 30*
(for each of these little garments)
150 g 8-ply, either plain or brushed yarn
5 mm and 3.25 mm needles

FUNTIME 1
You can use the Duet Valisa pattern (above) for Funtime 1, the yellow jumper. The back and front are knitted with the same number of sts, the bands are the same and so is the neckband. Here are the patterns for the decorations.

Green branch
Following the pattern for the tie bow from Love-in-the-mist (page 16), cast on enough sts in green wool for the size of branch you prefer. If using very thick mohair yarn you will only need to cast on, turn and cast off, but if you have used 8-ply wool, I suggest that you knit 1 row, then cast off.

Swing
Using a scrap of brown wool, knit the ropes the same way as the branch. Knit them to the length you want. In this case 8-ply wool works best.

Seat
Using a scrap of 8-ply brown wool, cast on enough sts for the little girl to sit on. Knit 3 rows then cast off.

Arms, legs and face
These are very easy to knit, to whatever size you require. For the arms and legs, cast on the required length in pale pink wool, and cast off.
For the face, knit the basic square pattern until you have 10 or 12 sts, and then cast off.

Hat, skirt and shoes
Knit the basic square to 16 sts, then cast off, for the hat and skirt. The shoes are little basic squares; inc up to 7 sts, then cast off.

All of the decorations are sewn on with running stitch. Make sure you do not pull your work or it will gather and won't sit flat. When I cast off I always leave a tail of wool for sewing the decorations on.
You may see that I have used it to gather the hat before I sewed it onto the garment.

One thing to remember—sew the arms *behind* the swing ropes. During one of my first lessons, when I went out to demonstrate Squareknits at a school, I was told, 'You have the hands on wrong, Mrs Guilford, you don't hold a swing like that.' There was no answer to that. Children are our best critics. After that I made sure that everyting was checked!

FUNTIME 2

Knit 2 squares alike.

Cast on 2 sts and knit the basic square, inc to 70 sts.

Knit the halfway row.

Knit the basic square dec. Fasten off.

Sew both shoulders together. Around the armhole pick up 46 sts and knit 6 to 8 rows in gt st. To pick up sts evenly, start at the shoulder, using a double-pointed needle, then put them all together to knit.

Knit the lower bands for the front and back from Love-in-the-mist (page 16).

The decorations have been knitted like Funtime 1, except that the face has been turned around, using the beginning as the nose.

For the flower, follow the instructions under Poppy on page 37, adding a centre as shown on page 63.

Domino jumper

Materials   *Illustrated on page 31*

400 g 8-ply for M

100 g 8-ply for con A

5 mm needles

Back

Knit 4 squares, 2 in M and 2 in con A.

Knit each basic square pattern to 40 sts.

Knit the halfway row.

Then finish off the basic square dec.

Front

Knit 4 squares for the back, 2 in M and 2 in con A.

For the flaps knit two extra basic pieces, inc to 18 sts. Knit one straight row, then cast off.

Sew the squares tog with the two con A squares at the top, for both the back and the front. Sew up one shoulder seam for 6 to 7 cm. Then pick up 54 sts evenly around the neck and knit for 8 rows. Cast off loosely.

Sew the little flaps on the front neatly, sewing with the right side facing. If you sew them on from the back they may not fall the right way.

Pick up and knit the back and front bands in M, using the pattern from Love-in-the-mist (page 16).

Sleeves

This garment uses the basic batwing pattern for the sleeves —see page 10.

Knit the basic batwing pattern from 2 sts until you have 55 sts on your needle. Now knit the wrist, with 55 sts on the dec side, and 56 sts on the inc side. Knit for 18 rows.

Knit the halfway row.

Now you will inc at the wrist while dec the other side. Knit this way for 18 rows, on 55 sts and 56 sts.

Knit the basic batwing dec.

Fasten off.

When you sew the sleeve in, the seam will be on the top of the arm, not underneath it. Sew the seams carefully, as I have found that it is easy to get uneven.

I have not specified wristbands in this pattern, but as the wearer's arms get longer one can undo a little bit of the seam and knit one on in k1, p1 rib. It is also easy to make the garment a little longer by undoing the side seam and the cast-off row and knitting a few more rows. Children seem to grow up rather than outwards at this stage, and these are great garments to accommodate that.

For the decorative spots, knit a number of small flower centres, inc to 8 sts before decreasing and sewing up (see page 63).

Two versions of Liquorice Showers, in the multiple colours of
the pattern, and very effective basic black (page 36)

The colour swatches show the pretty stitch used for the Lacy White jumper in closer detail

Back view of the Lacy White jumper from page 36, identical to the front.

Joanna models the glowing Poppy design (page 37), guaranteed to brighten up a dull day

Liquorice showers jumper

Illustrated on page 34

Materials
650 g 8-ply wool (100 g light grey, 100 g bright pink, 450 g black)
4.5 mm and 3.25 mm needles

Front (4 alike)

This pattern is based on half squares, which start with 3 sts and inc to 90 sts. Although you are still knitting the basic square watch the pattern carefully as it is a little different.

Cast on 3 sts.
Knit 1 row.
K1, m1, p1, k1.
Change to pink, k1, m1, knit to end.
K1, m1, (keep the middle st as a p1), knit to end.
With grey, k1, m1, knit to end of row.
Next row, k1, m1, k to the middle st, p1, knit to end.
With black k1, m1, knit to end.
Next row, k1, m1, knit to middle st, p1, knit to end.

Continue in this manner in the colour sequence:
   10 pink, 2 grey, 2 black, 2 pink;
   10 grey, 2 black, 2 pink, 2 grey;
   10 black, 2 pink, 2 grey, 2 black;
   10 pink, 2 grey, 2 black, 2 pink;
   10 grey.

Cast off 2 panels.
With the other two panels, leave the sts on the needles for the lower band on one, and on the other for the neckband.

Lower band

Change to 3.25 mm needles, and in black knit 1 row, then rib for 9 rows, casting off on the 10th row.

Neckband

Knit 13 rows in rib. Cast off.

Back (4 alike)

Working in black, knit the basic square inc to 90 sts, casting off 2 of these 4 panels and on the other 2 knitting bands to match the front.

Sleeves

Knitting with black and using the basic square pattern, inc to 90 sts.
Knit the halfway row then knit the basic dec.
Fasten off.

Sleeve bands

Wrong side facing and using 3.25 mm needles, pick up 44 sts.
Knit 1 row.
In rib work 4 rows.
Now knit 1 row in pink.
Rib 1 row in pink.
Knit 1 row in grey.
Rib 1 row in grey.
Knit 1 row in black.
Rib 1 row in black.
Repeat this colour sequence once more.
Rib 3 rows in black. Cast off.

Sew all the pieces together and you have a very pretty garment. It looks very effective in one colour also—see the photographs.

Lacy white jumper

Illustrated on page 35

Materials
600 g of 8-ply wool
5 mm and 3.25 mm needles

Front and back

Cast on 2 sts and knit the basic square, inc to 16 sts.
Start the lacy pattern, which is a 1-row pattern. Still knitting the basic inc, knit *m1, sl 1, k1, psso*, repeat to end.
Continue knitting this way to 59 sts.
Knit 6 rows in plain gt st, remembering to inc (65 sts).
Knit 12 rows in pattern (77 sts).
Knit 6 rows in gt st (83 sts).
Knit another 12 rows in pattern (95 sts).
Knitted in gt st, the next row is the halfway row.
Continue with the basic square dec.
Knit 6 rows of garter st.
Knit 16 rows of pattern.
Continue, alternating 6 rows of gt st, 16 rows of pattern, until you have finished the basic square dec. Fasten off.

Sleeves

Knit the basic batwing inc in the lacy pattern, knitting to 60 sts.
Still in lacy pattern continue the basic batwing, knitting the wrist for 22 or 24 rows for one side and the same number of rows for the other side of the wrist. Knit one straight row and then finish the basic batwing dec. Fasten off.

Lower bands
Pick up 80 sts from the front, using 3.25 mm needles. Knitting in k1, p1 rib, knit for 18 rows. Cast off on the 19th row.
Make the back band the same way.

Neckband
Sew one shoulder tog, pick up 80 sts on 3.25 mm needles and knit in k1, p1 rib for 12 rows. Cast off.

Wristbands
Using 3.25 mm needles again, pick up sts evenly around the cuff *before* you sew the sleeve in. This makes it easier to work.
The number of sts will depend on how many rows you knitted for the wrist.
If, after you have knitted 2 rows, it looks as if you have too many sts go back and pick up fewer. Even though I have been knitting this way for years, I still have to resort to such tactics.
Sew your garment together. I hope you enjoy wearing it, as it is so comfortable. (The swatches show you the same pattern in other colours.)

Poppy jumper

Materials   *Illustrated on page 35*
500 g brushed wool
50 g brushed red wool for the flower
scrap of wool for the leaves (use the same wool if possible)
5 mm needles

Front and back
Cast on and knit the basic square pattern until you have 80 sts.
Knit the halfway row.
Knit the basic square dec, then fasten off.

Sleeves
Knit the basic batwing pattern inc to 60 sts. Knit the wrist on these 60 sts, knitting 18 rows. I suggest putting a marker here, using a different coloured wool, to help you count the rows for the wrist.
Knit another 18 rows, inc at the wrist side this time where you were dec before, still working with 60 sts.
Finish the basic square dec. Fasten off.

Back and front bands
You can knit the bands from Love-in-the-mist (page 16), knitting in gt st or k1, p1 rib.

Sleeve bands
Pick up the sts around the cuff evenly, and knit in either gt st or rib. With this sleeve you can do without the bands—as the wearer grows, just undo a little bit of the seam and knit a band on.

Collar
This pattern is very simple:
Sew one shoulder together, pick up 60 sts on 6 mm needles and knit for 7 or 8 cm. Cast off.
With this jumper you now have a choice of collars, and may like to choose one of the others.

Making up
Sew all the seams together, remembering that with the basic batwing the seam is on top of the arm, not underneath.

Poppy flower
Knit 4 basic squares in red up to 14 or 16 sts, then knit 4 straight rows to make a neat curve for the centre of the petal. Knit the basic dec and fasten off.
Knit a yellow basic square up to 7 sts for a small centre or 8 sts for the bigger size. See page 63 for making up the centre.
For the stem, cast on sts to the length you want and then cast off.
For the leaf, knit a basic square inc to the same number of sts you used for the flower petals (14 or 16), then cast off.

Sarah's little fluffy dog Rita tones nicely with the natural tones of the Lichen jumper (page 40)

Sarah in a Harlequin jumper, made special with an extra touch of contrast colour (page 40)

Amethyst's glowing tones (page 40) set off
Joanna's fair hair and skin

Ranks of 'caterpillar' ridges march across
front and back of the Caterpillar jumper
(page 41)

Harlequin

Illustrated on page 38

Materials
600 g 8-ply wool for M
200 g 8-ply wool for con A
100 g 8-ply wool for con B
5 mm and 4 mm needles

This is a very easy pattern to knit and looks lovely in any colour combination.

Con A squares (6 alike)
Knit the basic square inc to 30 sts. Knit the halfway row. Knit the basic square dec. Fasten off.

Con A squares (4 alike)
Knit the basic square inc to 30 sts. Knit the halfway row. Leave these sts on spare needles or stitch holders for the sleeve bands.

M squares (8 alike)
Knit the basic square inc to 30 sts. Knit the halfway row. Finish off the basic square dec. Fasten off.

M squares (4 alike)
Knit the basic square inc to 30 sts. Cast off 8 sts and complete the halfway row.
Leave these sts for the neckband.

Con B squares (4 alike)
Knit the basic square inc to 30 sts. Knit the halfway row. Leave these sts for the lower bands.

Waist bands
Sew all the squares neatly together, leaving a seam open so that you can knit the bands backwards and forwards. Make bands in k1, p1 rib for 4 rows in con B, 4 rows in con A, and 4 rows in M. Cast off.

Wristbands
To knit the wristbands back and forth you have to once again leave a seam open. On the first row knit 2 sts tog evenly along the row until you have 44 sts (that is, you have dec 16 sts).
Knit in k1, p1 rib for 16 rows, fewer if you want. Cast off.

Neckband
Put all neckband stitches on the needle, making sure that the cast-off stitches are in the shoulder position (88 sts). Decrease evenly on the first row (every 3 sts), until you have 58 sts. Knit in rib for 6 rows, casting off on the 7th. Fasten off.

Sew the remaining seams neatly.

Lichen jumper

Illustrated on page 38

Materials
600 g natural dyed wool
5 mm and 6 mm needles

Back and front
Knit the basic square inc to 80 sts. Knit the halfway row. Knit the basic square dec. Fasten off.

Back and front bands
Pick up and knit in k2, p2 rib (78 sts), and knit for 14 rows. Cast off.

Sleeves
Knit the basic square inc on the first st, as in the basic pattern, **but at the same time knit the lacy pattern *k1, m1, k2 tog***.
Knit the basic inc, *k1, m1, k2 tog* to end of row, until you have 78 sts.
Knit the halfway row in lacy pattern.
Working the basic dec, and still knitting the lacy pattern, finish the square. Fasten off.

Collar
Sew up one shoulder seam for 6 to 7 cm. With 6 mm needles, pick up 70 sts, knitting back and forth in the lacy pattern until work measures 15 cm. Cast off.

Sew the remaining seams together.

Amethyst jumper

Illustrated on page 39

Materials
400 g 8-ply wool in purple
50 g 8-ply wool in dark amethyst
50 g 8-ply wool in light amethyst
5 mm needles

Back
Knit the basic square in purple, inc to 76 sts.
Knit the halfway row, then knit the basic square dec. Fasten off.

Front
Knit a basic square, beginning with purple.
Knit to 18 sts.

Changing to light amethyst, knit the basic inc and knit to end of row.

On the row back, knit the basic inc and the next 4 sts, then p10, turn, k10, turn, p10, knit to the end of the row. This is how you knit the 'lozenge'.

Change back to the main shade and knit 8 rows.

Each time you change to amethyst to knit the lozenge you will have more sts. Always knit one straight row with the right side facing, then, as long as you remember that 10 sts make the lozenge, you can make your own design.

Knit to 76 sts, knit the halfway row, then the basic dec, adding streamers and lozenges as you go. Fasten off.

Sleeves

Knitting the basic batwing, inc to 50 sts. Knit the wrist over 16 rows, one way, and 16 rows the other, then knit the basic dec.

Put in lozenge stripes as you go.

Back and front bands

Pick up 68 sts and knit in k1, p1 rib for 14 rows for both front and back. Cast off.

Sleeve bands

Pick up 48 sts and knit in k1, p1 rib for 16 rows. Cast off.

Sew up all the seams. You may wish to add a collar. Whichever one you choose, leave a shoulder seam open while you knit the collar, sewing up when you have finished.

Caterpillar jumper

Materials   *Illustrated on page 39*
250 g 8-ply wool for M
50 g 8-ply wool for con A
50 g 8-ply wool for con B
4.5 mm and 3.25 mm needles

Front and back

Working with the M colour and the basic square inc, cast on 3 sts.

Row 1: knit 3 sts.
Row 2: inc, p1, k1 (4 sts).
Row 3: inc, knit to the end.
Row 4: inc, rep row 2.
Row 5: inc, rep row 3.
Continue in M in this pattern until you have knitted 12 rows (14 sts).
Change to con A, knit 1 row (still basic square inc).

Next row: k5, p1. Continue like this, making sure that the purl sts are evenly spaced between the previous 'caterpillar' (purl) sts. Look closely at the photograph to check the positions of the caterpillars.

Continue until you have knitted 12 rows.

Change to con B. Still knitting the basic inc, continue until 4 rows completed.

Knit the halfway row.

Continuing the basic square dec and still knitting with con B, continue until you have knitted the 12 rows.

Maintain these stripes until you have finished the basic dec. Fasten off.

Sleeves

Knitting the basic square inc using M, work to 51 sts.

Knit the halfway row.

Finish off the basic square dec. Fasten off.

Front and back bands

Knitting with M wool, with wrong side facing, pick up 35 sts.

Next row, *k1, inc in next st*, rep * to * end, k1 (52 sts).

Rib for 7 rows. Cast off.

Sleeve bands

Knitting with M wool, using 3.25 mm needles, and with the wrong side facing, pick up 25 sts.

K3, inc, rep * to * to last 2 sts, k2 (34 sts).

Rib 1 row.
Change to con B, knit 1 row.
Rib 1 row.
Change to con A, knit 1 row.
Rib 1 row.
Change to M, and knit 1 row.
Rib 2 rows.
Cast off.

Neckband (front and back alike)

With wrong side facing, using M wool, pick up 34 sts.

Inc into every st along the row (68 sts).

Rib 7 rows.

Cast off.

Sew the sleeves in, then all the side seams. Join the shoulder seam for about 5 cm. It will sit neatly if you do so.

This stripe pattern looks good in a great range of colour combinations.

Squareknit rugs—the first one, in glowing jewel colours, follows the pattern on page 44; the other one is based loosely on the Liquorice Showers pattern (page 36) with deep crocheted edges and luxurious tassels

Nautical sweater, featuring the chevron stripe (page 45)

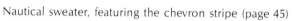

Sarah and John playing in the garden wearing All-Rounder from page 45 and Leather Tassels from page 49

Seventeen Squares (page 44)

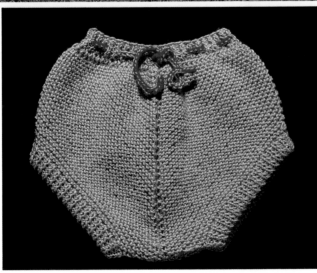

Toddler's romper pants with doubled leg bands and cord tie (page 44)

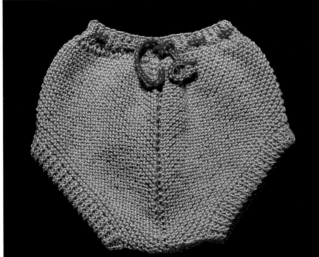

Toddler's romper pants

Illustrated on page 43

Materials
100 g 8-ply wool
4.5 mm, 4 mm and 3.25 mm needles

Front and back (4 pieces alike)
With 4.5 mm needles, knit the basic square inc to 46 sts.
The pattern now changes to the basic rectangle.
First row: inc, knit to the end (47 sts).
Dec, knit to the end (46 sts).
Repeat these 2 rows until the work measures 23 cm (on the inc side).
Continue to dec at the beg of each row until the dec on the 23 cm side measures 2.5 cm, and you have 38 sts on the needle. These 38 sts go onto spare needles or stitch holders for the leg bands.

Join centre front, centre back and one side seam. (Follow the diagram if the pattern seems confusing.)
With 3.25 mm needles, pick up 88 sts along waist edge, and knit 1 row.
Knit in k1, p1 rib, work 3 rows.
Make ribbonholes (rib 2, m1, k2 tog,) to the end.
Rib 3 rows.
Cast off with 4 mm needles.

Leg bands
Take 76 sts from the spare needles or stitch holders. Using 3.25 mm needles, rib for 14 rows.
Cast off loosely on the same needles.

Sew up the crutch and the remaining side seam.
Turn the leg bands so they are doubled, and sew inside.
Make a cord for the waistband. Thread through, and tie.

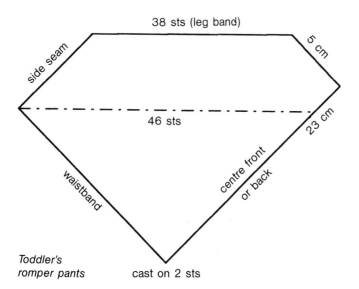

38 sts (leg band)
side seam
5 cm
46 sts
23 cm
waistband
centre front or back

Toddler's romper pants   cast on 2 sts

Squareknit rug

Illustrated on page 42

Materials
You can use up all your scraps for articles like this, or purchase special colours
3.75 mm needles

Knit the basic square inc to 72 sts.
Knit the halfway row.
To make the first pattern in the photographs, knit the basic dec in a shade of the wool you used first.
You are limited here only by your imagination, and the quantity of wool you have available.

Using black wool, double crochet around each square first, then pick up top loop from each square and double crochet to join.

The second photograph shows a rug based loosely on the Liquorice Showers jumper pattern (page 36). Other patterns could also be adapted to rug format with little trouble.

Seventeen squares

Illustrated on page 43

Here are a few ideas for using up spare squares, which may have been knitted as tension checks, or just for something to do. Just one thing—they must all be the same size, knitted from the basic square to 30 sts.

One square
Fold the square in half, and sew along the top and down the long side, leaving an opening at one end.
Turn so the seam is down the centre back.
Say the measurement across the top is 6 cm. With a threaded needle start 3 cm down the side and sew diagonally up to the centre top seam, using a running stitch. Gather it up, to make an ear. Do the same on the other side, sewing down 3 cm to the outside.
The next step is to pad the body with a soft material. Do not sew the lower seam yet, as you may like to use more padding.
Measure down from the tip of the ear 7 cm. Wrap a contrast wool tightly around the body to make a head. Tie this so that it won't come undone.
Pad the lower body with extra material if necessary, then sew up the seam.
Sew on features such as eyes, nose and whiskers, and you have a cat.

Two squares

With 2 squares knitted from the basic pattern to 30 sts, make a little pair of Jester Slippers, baby size (see page 16).

Six squares

Sew 6 squares together into a cube, leaving 1 seam open. Pad it and you have turned it into a ball, making a lovely soft toy for a small child. Pop a jingle bell in the centre if you like.

Eight squares

Knit 6 complete squares from the basic pattern to 30 sts, knit 2 more through to the basic dec, until you have 20 sts on your needle. These sts go into the neckband of a little V-neck tank top.

Go to the pattern Peach Parfait on page 25 and knit that neckband, though with 61 sts rather than 91.

Before you sew the side seams, pick up 45 sts evenly on the front of the garment, and knit 8 rows in gt st. Cast off. Knit the same band for the back and then sew all the remaining seams.

All-rounder jumper

Materials   *Illustrated on page 43*
500 g 8-ply wool
5 mm needles

This garment is made from just 4 squares.

Back and front (alike)

Knitting the basic square pattern inc to 94 sts.
Knit the halfway row.
Knit the basic dec. Fasten off.

Sleeves

Knit the basic square inc to 80 sts.
Knit the halfway row.
Knit the basic dec. Fasten off.

Front and back bands

Pick up 88 sts evenly, and knit in rib for 12 rows. Cast off.

The sleeves can be turned back with or without bands. If you are going to have bands, pick up and knit 44 sts, knitting in rib for 14 rows. Cast off.

For the neck band you now have a choice of several. If at any time you are in doubt about which to choose, look at a pattern that has the same number of sts.

Sew up seams.

Nautical sweater

Note that this pattern uses both squareknits and conventional knits.

Materials   *Illustrated on page 42*
200 g navy wool, 8-ply
50 g white wool, 8-ply
50 g red wool, 8-ply
5 mm and 4 mm needles

Back and front

Knit the basic square pattern inc to 80 sts with navy wool.
Knit the halfway row.
Knit the basic square dec. Fasten off.

Back and front bands

Using 4 mm needles, pick up 78 sts and work in k1, p1 rib for 14 rows. Cast off.

Sleeves

I am a great fan of chevron knitting. I have knitted these sleeves in a simple garter stitch pattern. If you find the pattern difficult, you can knit 4 basic squares instead.

Chevron pattern (5 mm needles)

With navy wool, cast on 68 sts and knit 2 rows.
Start the pattern with navy.
Row 1: k1, k2 tog, *k5, m1, k1, m1, k5, sl 1, k2 tog, psso*, rep from * to * to the last 14 sts, k5, m1, k1, m1, k5, sl 1, k1, psso, k1.
Row 2: k1, p1, *k5, k1 tbl, k1, k1 tbl, k5, p1*, rep from * to * to last st, k1.
Change to white, and repeat these 2 rows.
Knit in this pattern until you have knitted 7 white stripes and 8 navy. Cast off.

Sew the shoulders, then put the sleeves in, and then sew all the side seams.

Red tie

This is knitted using the basic rectangle pattern, on 16 sts, until the work measures 90 cm. Finish with the basic dec. Fasten off.

You can knit a smaller strip exactly the same way on 16 sts to go around the tie to keep it together. Sew the seam and thread the tie through.

I do hope that you have tried to knit the chevron. Once you have learnt it you will find yourself using it a lot.

Emma models Red Glow (page 48), one of a number of jumpers incorporating the streamer and lozenge stripe

The pretty Bulrush jumper (page 48) features streamer and lozenge stripes in sleeves and waistband

The multicoloured stripes of Little Pet are particularly effective on a black background (page 48)

The Rosemary cardigan, earthy in multistripes of natural-dyed wool (page 48)

Red glow jumper

Materials   *Illustrated on page 46*
150 g 14-ply blue wool
350 g 14-ply red wool
6 mm needles

Front and back
Cast on, starting with the blue wool, and knitting the basic pattern inc to 19 sts.
Now change to red, and knit the 'lozenge streamer'. Starting with the inc, knit to the end of the row.
Knit the inc, k15, turn, p10, turn, k10, turn, p10, turn, knit to end of row.
Change back to blue and knit 6 rows, remembering the inc.
Change to red and knit another stripe. You will have more sts, and could put in two lozenges, but at this stage I would just knit one.
Continue knitting inc to 60 sts.
Knit the halfway row.
Now knit the basic dec with red, making the stripes in blue.
Dec to 20 sts, and finish off the basic square without making any stripes.

Sleeves
Knit the basic square inc to 58 sts. You can put in the lozenge streamers as in the front, or leave the sleeves plain.
Knit the halfway row, then finish the basic dec. Fasten off.

Sleeve bands
Pick up 44 sts, and in k2, p2 rib knit for 10 rows, cast off.

Back and front bands
Pick up 52 sts, and knit in k2, p2 rib for 12 rows. Cast off.

Neckband
Knit the neckband pattern for Caterpillar (page 41).

Bulrush jumper

Materials   *Illustrated on page 46*
500 g 8-ply wool for M
100 g 8-ply wool for con A
5 mm and 4 mm needles

Front and back
Knit the basic square in M, on 5 mm needles, to 84 sts.
Knit the halfway row, then knit the basic dec. Fasten off.

Bands (back and front alike)
Pick up 80 sts on 5 mm needles. In M, knit 6 rows in gt st.

Knit the lozenge streamer in con A (refer to Red Glow jumper, page 48). Knit 6 rows in M, another streamer in con A, and 5 more rows in M. Cast off on the 6th row.

Sleeves
Knit the basic square inc to 80 sts. At the same time work in the lozenge streamers, knitting 10 rows between each one. Have them spaced so that they do not fall one above another. Knit the halfway row, then the rest of the basic square dec. Fasten off.

Sleeve bands
Pick up and knit 38 sts on 4 mm needles; work in k1, p1 rib for 16 rows. Cast off.

Collar
Sew 1 shoulder before you pick up the sts.
Pick up 70 sts in M, and knit in gt st for 12 rows. (If you have knitted this to fit an adult, pick up 90 sts.)
Put in a streamer in con A, and then knit for 5 rows. Cast off on the 6th row.
Sew the side seams, the neckband, and along the remaining shoulder.

Little pet jumper

Materials   *Illustrated on page 47*
400 g black 8-ply wool
25 g various colours for stripes, a good way to use up scraps
5 mm needles

Back and front
This is another way of using lozenge streamers, which looks great with the black background.
Knit the basic square inc to 70 sts, knitting in the streamers with 8 rows between.
Knit the halfway row, then the basic dec, still putting in the stripes. Cast off.

Sleeves (4 alike)
Knit the basic square up to 35 sts, matching the stripes if you can. Knit the halfway row, then the basic dec and fasten off.

Back and front bands
Pick up 65 sts if you are going to knit the band in gt st, 70 sts for a k1, p1 rib.
Knit 13 rows and cast off on the 14th.

Sew all the seams together. Make a little tassel of coloured wools and sew to the neck. Remember to sew the shoulders together for 5 or 6 cm.

Rosemary cardigan

Materials   *Illustrated on page 47*
100 g of natural-dyed 8-ply wool, cinnamon
100 g each of 4 contrasting colours in 4-ply
5 mm and 3.25 mm needles

Back

Knitting the basic square pattern, using the 8-ply cinnamon wool and 5 mm needles, knit to 20 sts.
The next row, change to the first contrast (4-ply), and to 3.25 mm needles. **It is very important to remember that you are still knitting the basic square inc.** Change to st st.
The next 10 rows are the pattern.
Row 1: After your basic inc, inc into every st along the row (40 sts).
Row 2: *Basic inc, and p to the end of the row (41 sts).
Row 3: Inc, then k to the end (42 sts).
Row 4: Inc, p to end (42 sts).
Row 5: Inc, k to end* (44 sts).
Rows 6, 7, 8: Rep the rows from * to * until 8 rows have been knitted.
Row 9: **(Remember you have knitted in st st, from the row of incs, 8 rows. That means that you have 4 sts extra, on each side, from the basic inc.)**
Row 10: Knit your basic inc, k4 and k2 tog, k2 tog to the last 4 sts (28 sts).
Rows 11-16: Knit the next 6 rows in 8-ply on the 5 mm needles.
Continue knitting these 16 pattern rows until you have 80 sts. Knit the halfway row and then finish the basic dec. Fasten off.

Back band

Pick up 78 sts on 5 mm needles and knit in gt st. Knit either one colour or in stripes until you have worked 14 rows. Cast off.

Sleeves

Knit the basic square, and the pattern, until you have 78 sts. Knit the halfway row, and finish off the square. Fasten off.

Sleeve bands

Pick up and knit 40 sts in gt st on 5 mm needles. Knit to match the back band. Cast off.

Fronts

Put buttonholes on the right side as you knit.
Knit the basic rectangle, in the pattern, until you have 40 sts. Match the colours if you can. On the 40 sts, knit until the side measurements are even. Dec the basic rectangle until you have 24 sts. Leave these on a spare needle for the neckband.
Knit the other front the same, omitting the buttonholes. (I always like to knit the left side of a cardigan first so I can measure the finished length and place the buttonholes evenly on the right side).

Front lower bands

Pick up and knit 38 sts in gt st on 5 mm needles, knitting stripes to match the back at the side seam. Make a buttonhole in the right band. Knit the same number of rows. Cast off.

Collar (both sizes of needle)

Sew the shoulders together, and with the 24 sts from the left front on the spare needle, knit to the back of the neck, pick up 24 sts, then knit the last 24 sts from the spare needle on the right front.
Knit 6 rows in the cinnamon, then knit the 16 rows of the pattern. Cast off.

Leather tassels jumper

Materials   *Illustrated on page 43*
400 g 8-ply wool
5 m fine leather thonging, any colour
4.5 mm needles

Back

Knit the basic square inc to 66 sts.
Knit the halfway row, then finish off the basic dec. Fasten off.

Front

Knit the basic square inc to 66 sts. Knit the halfway row. Knitting the basic dec, start knitting the thonging in with the wool. Say you are down to 64 sts. Knit 22 sts, then for the next 15 sts knit the thonging with the wool. (Before you start knitting leave about a 3 cm tail.) Then finish the row with wool.
Bring the thonging to the right side and cut off about 3 cm. It will not come undone. Continue in this way, knitting the thonging in evenly. (The first bit you put in may go wrong because you have twisted it with the wool. Try again.)
Finish the basic square dec and fasten off.

Sleeves (4 alike)

Knit the basic square inc to 40 sts. Knit the halfway row, then finish the basic dec. Fasten off.
Sew in the sleeves, and the side seams. This garment has no bands on the lower edges. They could be added as the child grows to make the jumper larger.

Neck band

Knit a Plunket shoulder on this garment with 60 sts.
Be very careful not to rub the knitted-in thonging when you wash this jumper, as it may be spoiled.

These colourful ponchos demonstrate the versatility of the
Poncho pattern (page 52)

Two versions of the Squareknit Coat in 14-ply and 8-ply wool (page 52)

The Squareknit Jacket (page 53) in a luxurious brown mohair yarn

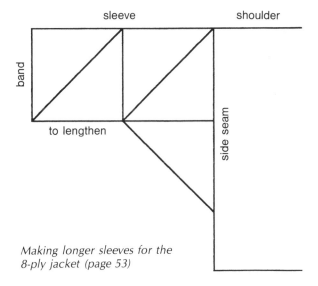

Making longer sleeves for the 8-ply jacket (page 53)

Ponchos 1 and 2

PONCHO 1

Materials   *Illustrated on page 50*
100 g 4-ply white wool
100 g 4-ply lemon wool
3.25 mm needles

Knit 6 (alike)
Knit the basic square pattern with lemon wool to 40 sts.
Knit the halfway row.
Change to white, and finish the basic square. Fasten off.

Knit 2 (alike)
In lemon wool, knit the basic square inc to 40 sts. Leave these on a spare needle.
Knit the second piece the same.
Pick up 80 sts altogether, and work 2 rows in k1, p1 rib.
Next row in st st, *k2, m1, k2 tog*. Rep * to * to end of row.
Back to k1, p1 rib and knit 2 rows.
Cast off.

Sew pieces together and crochet a cord to go around the neck in the ribbonholes. Knot a fringe around the lower edge in lemon wool. If you reverse the colourways on the poncho, make the fringe white.

PONCHO 2

Materials   *Illustrated on page 50*
100 g 12-ply wool
5 mm needles

Back
Knit the basic square inc to 60 sts.
Knit the halfway row.
Work the basic dec until there are 24 sts left. Put them on a spare needle.

Front
Knit the basic inc to 48 sts.
Now knit the basic inc on one side, and on the other knit straight (no shaping) for 12 rows (6 ridges). The straight knitting edge is the neck. Now, knitting the halfway row and starting from the neck, cast off 20 sts, and knit to the end of the row.
Knit the basic dec now. The next row is dec and knit to the end, then cast on 20 sts.
Knitting straight on the neck edge for 12 rows, continue knitting the basic dec until you have finished the square. Fasten off.

Neck band
Pick up 12 sts from neck edge, 20 sts across the back, and another 12 sts from the other side of the neck.
Knit in gt st for 2 rows. Knit the row of ribbonholes as in the first pattern, knit 2 more rows of gt st, and cast off. Make 4 short cords for the front and attach them to the poncho. Sew the seams over the shoulder.

A fringe can be added if you like.

Squareknit coats

LONG COAT IN 14-PLY

When I knit myself a coat in any of the heavier wools, I knit the back, then the fronts, sew the shoulder seams up to where they are needed, then I hang the garment on a broom handle for a day or two. (Hanging it on a coathanger only drops the shoulders, and this can be very offputting.) The broomhandle lets the coat drop evenly, so that when I am ready to knit the bands, I can see where a stitch or two less might be needed. If you are in doubt about all of this, the safest thing is to knit the garment a few centimetres shorter than your measurements indicate.

Materials   *Illustrated on page 51*
900 g 14-ply wool
6.5 mm and 4.5 mm needles
6 or 7 large buttons

Back (6.5 mm needles)
Knit the basic rectangle inc to 86 sts.
Continue on these 86 sts until the inc side seam measures 90 cm.
Finish knitting the basic rectangle dec and fasten off.

Back band (4.5 mm needles)
Pick up 60 sts, and knit in k1, p1 rib for 16 rows. Cast off.

Fronts (6.5 mm needles)
Knit 2.
Knit the basic rectangle to 32 sts.
Knit the rectangle inc pattern until the work measures the same as the back side seam, 90 cm.
Finish the basic dec, and fasten off.

Front lower bands (4.5 mm needles)
Pick up 30 sts and knit in k1, p1 rib for 16 rows. Cast off.

Centre front bands (4.5 mm needles)

Knitting the left side first, pick up 122 sts, and knit in k1, p1 rib for 6 rows. Cast off on the 7th row.

The right side will have the buttonholes. Knitting the left side first gives you a measurement for spacing the buttonholes evenly.

Pick up 122 sts, and knit 3 rows in k1, p1 rib. On the 4th row make the buttonholes. In 14-ply wool you have only to m1, k2 tog to make a buttonhole. When you knit back, it will look neat. Knit until you have 6 rows and cast off on the 7th row.

Sleeves (6.5 mm needles)

Knit the basic batwing pattern to 50 sts, then knit the wrist (24 rows, 7 cm for an average wrist).

Knit the halfway row, then knit for another 24 rows, finishing the batwing dec. Fasten off. There are no bands for the sleeves.

Pockets (6.5 mm needles)

Knit 2.

Cast on 10 sts, and knit the basic inc to 40 sts.
Knit the halfway row, then the basic dec to 30 sts.
Cast off firmly.

Neck band (put this on last)

Sew the shoulder seams up for 12 cm, pick up sts evenly around the neck on 4.5 mm needles, and knit for 6 rows.

Sew all the remaining seams, making sure to get the sleeves even, and sew the pockets on. They are for using, so put them where the wearer will find them comfortable. Sew the buttons on.

LONG COAT IN 8-PLY

Materials   *Illustrated on page 51*
700 g 8-ply wool
5 mm and 4 mm needles

Back (5 mm needles)

Knit the basic rectangle to 100 sts, then knit on 100 sts, until you have the length you require (waist to shoulder). Finish the basic rectangle pattern. Fasten off.

Fronts (5 mm needles)

Knit 2.
Knit the basic rectangle inc to 50 sts.
Knit on 50 sts until the work measures the same as the back side seam. Finish the basic dec.
Fasten off.

Back band (4 mm needles)

Pick up 80 sts in k1, p1 rib, knit 14 rows. Cast off.

Front bands (4 mm needles)

Pick up 46 sts in k1, p1 rib, knit 14 rows. Cast off.

Sleeves (5 mm needles)

There are two ways to knit the sleeve. As you have learnt the basic batwing, I am going to give you this version which looks exactly the same.

Knit the basic square inc to 43 sts, then knit the halfway row. Knit the basic square dec, and fasten off.

You will knit 6 of these squares, 3 for each sleeve.

If you want your garment with longer sleeves, knit 4 more squares. Use the diagram on the photo page as a guide for sewing the sleeves together. You may like the sleeves without bands. If so, leave one seam open so that you can knit back and forth after picking up the sts (44 sts) and knit for 14 rows. Cast off.

JACKET

Materials   *Illustrated on page 51*
600 g mohair yarn
6 mm and 4 mm needles

Back (6 mm needles)

Knit the basic rectangle inc to 84 sts. On these 84 sts work until you have 74 cm, then finish the basic dec.

Fronts (6 mm needles)

Knit the basic rectangle to 40 sts. Knit on 40 sts until your work measures the same as the back seam (74 cm). Finish the basic dec, and fasten off.

Sleeves (6 mm needles)

Knit the basic batwing pattern, to 58 sts. Knit the wrists for 7 cm on one side and 7 cm on the other, then finish the basic batwing pattern. Fasten off.

Sleeve bands (4 mm needles)

Picking up 42 sts, k1, p1 rib for 17 rows. Cast off on the 18th.

Sew the sleeves in, and sew up the side seams, then pick up 166 sts with 4 mm needles, across one front, the back, and the other front. Then knit for 9 rows, casting off on the 10th.

Front bands (4 mm needles)

Knit 2.
Pick up 82 sts and knit for 9 rows. Cast off on the 10th.

Neck band (4 mm needles)

Sew the shoulder seams.
Pick up 102 sts evenly, k1, p1 rib for 9 rows, and cast off on the 10th row.

Clouds (page 56) is knitted to fit an average ten-year-old

Apricot Haze (page 57) is a softly elegant jumper for an adult

Clouds jumper

Materials   *Illustrated on page 54*
500 g white 8-ply wool
250 g 8-ply wool in the following colours: N—navy, Wh—white, G-green, M—maroon, B—blue, T—tan, F—fawn, R—red, K—khaki, Gy—grey, O—orange, Ltb—light blue, Dkg—dark green, Bl—black, Ltg—light green. X is a bright colour of your choice.
5 mm needles

Back

With white knit the basic square inc to 79 sts. Knit the halfway row, then the basic square dec. Fasten off.

Sleeves (4 alike)

Knit the basic square in white inc to 45 sts. Knit the halfway row, then knit the basic square dec. Fasten off.

Front

With white wool, knit the basic square inc to 6 sts.
From now on I am only going to give you the number of sts with the colour changes. **You** must remember the basic inc and the basic dec. The other thing to remember is that **the even numbered rows** (as we are knitting in gt st) **will be inc**, then colour over colour exactly.

6th row: (You have 6 sts and have knitted them white.)
7th row: 3N, 4Wh
9th row: 5N, 4Wh
11th row: 6N, 5Wh
13th row: 8N, 5Wh
15th row: 10N, 5Wh
17th row: 10N, 7Wh
19th row: 6N, 6G, 7Wh
21st row: 7N, 8G, 6Wh
23rd row: 7N, 9G, 7Wh
25th row: 7N, 11G, 7Wh
27th row: 9M, 9G, 9Wh
29th row, 11M, 6G, 7Wh, 5N
31st row: 13M, 3G, 7Wh, 8N
33rd row: 7M, 7Wh, 9G, 10N
35th row: 5M, 18Wh, 12N
37th row: 8Ltb, 14Wh, 15N
39th row: 10Ltb, 7Wh, 8B, 14N
41st row: 12Ltb, 6Wh, 9B, 7N, 7T
43rd row: 13Ltb, 5Wh, 10B, 6N, 9T
45th row: 13Ltb, 6Wh, 10B, 6N, 10T
47th row: 13Ltb, 6Wh, 10B, 7N, 11T
49th row: 12Ltb, 11Wh, 7B, 6N, 13T
51st row: 8Ltb, 7Ltg, 10Wh, 9B, 17T
53rd row: 8Ltb, 11Ltg, 12Wh, 4B, 6T, 12Wh
55th row: 9Ltb, 15Ltg, 8Wh, 3B, 6T, 14Wh

57th row: 11R, 13Ltg, 12Wh, 6T, 15Wh
59th row: 14R, 8Ltg, 7Bl, 10Ltb, 6T, 14Wh
61st row: 18R, 7Ltg, 7Bl, 11Ltb, 7T, 11Wh
63rd row: 18R, 8Ltg, 8Bl, 12Ltb, 6T, 11Wh
65th row: 11R, 7N, 9Ltg, 10Bl, 10Ltb, 8T, 5Wh, 15Dkg
67th row: 11R, 8N, 8Ltg, 12Bl, 10Ltb, 6T, 5Wh, 7Dkg
69th row: 10R, 14N, 9Ltg, 8Gy, 9Ltb, 6T, 4Wh, 9Dkg
71st row: 6R, 5Wh, 14N, 9Ltg, 9Gy, 14Ltb, 3Wh, 11Dkg
73rd row: 6R, 6Wh, 15N, 8Ltg, 10Gy, 16Ltb, 11Dkg
75th row: 6R, 15Wh, 7N, 8K, 16Gy, 9Ltb, 14Dkg
77th row: 6R, 18Wh, 6N, 10K, 12Gy, 10Ltb, 15Dkg
79th row: 6R, 18Wh, 12N, 13K, 9Wh, 10Ltb, 11Dkg
Knit the halfway row.

Now for the dec.
79th row: 5R, 19Wh, 12N, 13K, 9Wh, 10Ltb, 10Dkg
77th row: 9B, 9G, 9Ltb, 7F, 13K, 12Wh, 18Ltb
75th row: 9B, 8G, 9Ltb, 7F, 13K, 13Wh, 16Ltb
73rd row: 10B, 9G, 6Ltb, 3F, 9Ltb, 10K, 8W, 8O, 3Ltb, 7Dkg
71st row: 8B, 11G, 5Ltb, 11F, 10K, 9Wh, 10O, 7Dkg
69th row: 6B, 12G, 5Ltb, 11F, 10K, 8N, 11O, 6Dkg
67th row: 4B, 12G, 5Ltb, 16F, 10K, 3Wh, 11O, 6Dkg
65th row: 3B, 17G, 17F, 12N, 11O, 5Dkg
63rd row: 2B, 15G, 10X, 9Wh, 11N, 12O, 4Dkg
61st row: 1B, 14G, 12X, 8Wh, 10N, 16O
59th row: 13G, 12X, 8Wh, 17N, 9O
57th row: 8T, 6Wh, 10X, 8Wh, 25N
55th row: 7T, 7Wh, 9X, 14Wh, 18N
53rd row: 5T, 8W, 9X, 14Wh, 17N
51st row: 7T, 8Wh, 8X, 15Wh, 13N
49th row: 7T, 7Wh, 9X, 14Wh, 12N
47th row: 6T, 5Wh, 15R, 10Wh, 11N
45th row: 4T, 5Wh, 15R, 10Wh, 11N
43rd row: 3T, 5Wh, 14R, 10Wh, 11N
41st row: 3T, 5Wh, 13R, 9Wh, 11N
39th row: 2T, 5Wh, 12R, 12Wh, 8N
37th row: 1T, 19Wh, 15G, 5Wh, 6N
35th row: 10W, 15G, 5Wh, 5N
33rd row: 8W, 15G, 5W, 5N
31st row: 6Wh, 15G, 5Wh, 5N
29th row: 7N, 12G, 10Wh
27th row: 7N, 11G, 9Wh
25th row: 10N, 7G, 8Wh
23rd row: 9N, 7G, 7Wh
21st row: 8N, 6G, 7Wh
19th row: 9N, 3G, 7Wh
17th row: 9N, 2G, 6Wh
15th row: 9N, 6Wh
13th row: 7N, 6Wh
11th row: 5N, 6Wh
9th row: 3N, 6Wh
7th row: 2N, 5Wh
5th row: 2N, 3Wh
3rd row: 1N, 2Wh
Fasten off the basic dec.

Clouds has the Plunket shoulder, but you may like to choose another collar.

The lower bands are from Love-in-the-mist (page 16). Knit these, then sew the seams.

Apricot haze jumper

Materials *Illustrated on page 55*
600 g 8-ply wool
5 mm and 3.25 mm needles

Back and front

Knit the basic square on 5 mm needles inc to 16 sts. Keep on inc, and knit in the pattern as follows.

Row 1: inc., k5, *k2 tog, m1, k1, m1, k2 tog*, k5 (17 sts).
Row 2 and alternate rows: Knit. Knit the basic inc before the halfway row and basic dec after.
Row 3: inc, k5, *k2 tog, m1, k3, m1, k2 tog*, k5 (19 sts).
Row 5: inc, k5, *k2 tog, m1, k5, m1, k2 tog*, k5 (21 sts).
Row 7: inc, k5, *k2 tog, m1, k7, m1, k2 tog*, k5 (23 sts).
Row 9: inc, k5, *k2 tog, m1, k9, m1, k2 tog*, k5 (25 sts).
Row 11: inc, k5, *k2 tog, m1, k11, m1, k2 tog*, k5 (27 sts).
Row 13: inc, k6, *m1, k2 tog, k11, k2 tog, m1*, k6 (29 sts).
Row 15: inc, k8, *m1, k2 tog, k9, k2 tog, m1*, k8 (31 sts).
Row 17: inc, k10, *m1, k2 tog, k7, k2 tog, m1*, k10 (33 sts).
Row 19: inc, k12, *m1, k2 tog, k5, k2 tog, m1*, k12 (35 sts).
Row 21: inc, k14, *m1, k2 tog, k3, k2 tog, m1*, k14, (37 sts).
Row 23: inc, k16, *m1, k2 tog, k1, k2 tog, m1*, k16,* (39 sts).
Row 24: As Row 2.

That is the middle diamond of the pattern. You continue to knit this right through the back and the front of the jumper (from the basic inc to the basic dec).

Now start the zigzag on either side of the diamond. The next row is the 25th and is in sections so you shouldn't get lost.

Row 25: Knit the basic inc, k9, k2 tog, m1, k7 (there will always be 7 sts between the zigzags, either side of the diamond), k2 tog, m1, k1, (put a coloured thread around the k1, to give yourself a guide until you get used to the pattern), m1, k2 tog, k7, m1, k2 tog, knit to the end.
As before all alternate rows are knitted with the inc.
Now continue following the pattern from * to *. That part will always be the same.
When you get to 7 sts plus 5, make another zigzag and continue until you have 98 sts.
Knit the halfway row in pattern.
Knit the basic dec in pattern until you have 16 sts, then knit without pattern until you have finished. Fasten off.

Back and front bands (3.25 mm needles)

Pick up 82 sts and knit in k1, p1 rib for 17 rows. On the 18th row cast off.

Sleeves

Knit the basic square on 5 mm needles inc to 86 sts.
Knit the halfway row, and dec down to 70 sts.
Across the next row knit the zigzags by dec, k10, k2 tog, m1, k7, k2 tog, m1, k7, k2 tog, to last 3 sts, k3.
Now, knitting the basic dec, follow the zigzag pattern from the back and front until you have 16 sts. If you have the pattern in the centre and want to finish it off, do so, as it will not alter the square. Fasten off.

Sleeve bands (3.25 mm needles)

Pick up 42 sts, and knit in k1, p1 rib for 15 rows. On the 16th row, cast off.

Sew a shoulder seam for 23 cm.

Neck band (3.25 mm needles)

Pick up 80 sts around the neck, and in k1, p1 rib knit for 6 rows. Now follow the pattern for the soft collar from Love-in-the-mist (page 17).

Sew in the sleeves, then all the remaining seams.

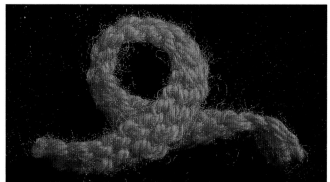

The tie bow for Love-in-the-mist (page 16) is but one use for this knitted strip, described on page 60

Picking up stitches illustrated with contrasting wool (page 60)

This jumper has been lengthened by the addition of matching rectangles (page 60)

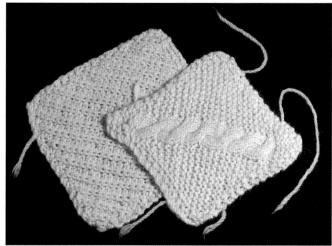

Swatches of Fisherman's Rib and Cable designs (page 60)

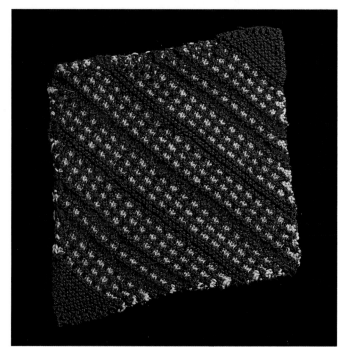

Mock Fair Isle knitting (page 60)

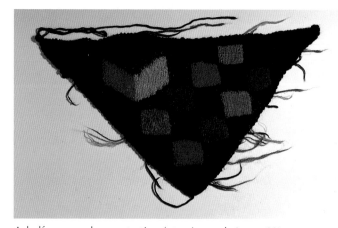

A half square demonstrating Intarsia work (page 60)

Emma, knitted in handspun wool, is based on the Windmill pattern (page 17)

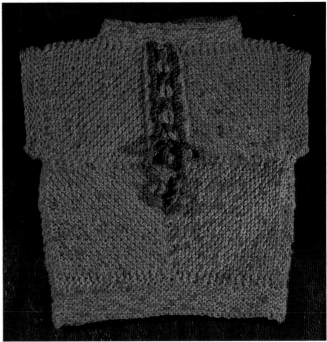

Orangeade (page 60)

Little V Neck Pullover (page 60)

A little tank top trimmed with a patch and a tie bow initial (page 60)

Versatile Child's Cardigan (page 60)

Miscellany and hints

Illustrated on page 58

Tie bow (for the collar of Love-in-the-mist, page 16)
Cast on 30 sts, turn and cast off.
This is used for all straight knitting—like the branch, the swing ropes, legs and arms and flower stems in the pattern Funtime (page 32).

Picking up stitches   *Illustrated on page 58*
Look at the photograph of picking up stitches. For the lower bands of a garment pick up the sts on the **inc edge**. If you pick up a st on every ridge remember that it takes two rows to make a ridge, so you will have to inc to get the sts required.

Changing needles with a change of ply

14-ply 6 mm, 6.5 mm
12-ply 6 mm, 5 mm
 8-ply 5 mm, 4.5 mm, 4 mm
 4-ply 3 mm, 3.75 mm, 3.5 mm
 3-ply 2.75 mm, 3 mm, 3.25 mm
 2 ply 2 mm, 2.75 mm

To lengthen a garment   *Illustrated on page 58*
1. Unpick the bands on the back and front. If the garment has been knitted in separate squares knit 4 more and sew them on to the lower ones. Put another band on now if you wish or use it for a later lengthening.
2. Unpick the bands and knit 2 basic rectangles, knitting them long enough to reach from side seam to side seam, and wide enough for the extra depth required.

Eyelets
A very quick way to make eyelets for a cord when you are knitting the basic square inc is to alternate the way you do it. If you knit the inc following the pattern, you will be knitting into the front and the back of the st. You can do this on one side, and on the other knit 1 stitch, pick up the loop between the next 2 sts, making a st, and knit to the end of the row. The next inc is the normal one, and so on alternately.

Plunket shoulder
Several garments can have this neckline. You may have knitted straight neckbands for the jumpers Caterpillar, Red Glow, Leather Tassels, Emma and Liquorice Showers. Before you sew the shoulders up you overlap the back neckband the width of the front neckband, making a double thickness, which makes the neck snug. You sew this small seam when putting the sleeves in.
Comet (page 24) has no bands at the neck; if you want to knit a Plunket shoulder for this jumper, knit 86 sts in k1, p1 rib for 8 rows or gt st a band on the back and front before you start.

Pattern swatches   *Illustrated on page 58*
These swatches are for knitting patterns that look comfortable. They can be knitted in any size of square as long as you remember a few ground rules.
Cable: I suggest that where you wish to use a cable, knit 4 smaller squares instead of 1 large one. On each square use no more than 6 sts width for the cable, with one purl st each side. When knitting the 2 squares that are to go into the neckband you will only need to dec down to the cable sts as these sts are for the neckband.
Fisherman's rib: Start once you get to 6 sts, and knit the dec down to 6 sts, knitting the rest of the square in gt st.
Mock Fair Isle: This is a very easy way to make colour changes, and looks very effective. Knit with the main colour for as many rows as required, then change to a contrast and knit k2, sl 1 or 2, to the end. On the row back purl, and either slip the slipped sts or knit them purlwise. This depends on the effect you want. The swatch photo has the two rows slipped.
Intarsia: This can look very effective on a dark background, and although slow it is possible as long as you remember to inc and dec.

Design suggestions   *Illustrated on pp. 59, 62*
Emma A little jumper knitted out of handspun wool which makes a good extra for cold days. The front is knitted in the Windmill pattern, and it has a Plunket shoulder.
Orangeade, knitted with 8 squares.
Little Tank Top, knitted with 2 large squares, 1 small, and the tie bow for the initial.
Little Vest, knitted with 1 large square for the back, and 2 basic rectangles for the fronts, with just a comfortable shoulder knitted before casting off.
Little V Neck Pullover, knitted with the basic batwing for the sleeves, 1 basic square for the back, and 2 basic rectangles for the fronts. Follow Peach Parfait (page 25) for the neckband.
Versatile Childs' Cardigan, a larger version of the Basic Baby's Garment (page 28); the back is 1 basic square, the fronts are 2 basic rectangles, and the sleeves are 2 basic squares. The bands are also from that pattern.
Twelve Squares, knitted from 12 basic squares. Sew seams up leaving the front seam open between the top 2 squares. The lower bands and neckbands have been crocheted.
Elegance: Pink, light grey, steel grey, white and a medium grey make a lovely colour combination. The measurements for this garment are from the pattern Apricot Haze (page 57).

Toys and housewares   *Illustrated on pp. 62–63*
All these items are made out of oddments of wool, using under 100 g, and are knitted on 4.5 mm needles unless otherwise stated.
Guyon the Cat: Knit the basic square inc to 40 sts. Knit the halfway row, then knit the basic square dec. Fasten off.

You can put the cat together like the one in Seventeen Squares (page 44) or like this:

Make 2 ears by knitting the basic pattern to 8 sts. Knit 2 halfway rows and cast off.

To put the cat together, fold the square in half, and sew the seam up the longer side. Across the back sew a running stitch, then gather. Make sure that this is secure so it doesn't come undone when you pad the body. Sew on the ears. Pad the body with something soft, and sew the other seam. Tie a thread around the top of the body to make the head. Use a different colour so that it can act as a scarf.

Martian: Made with 2 larger squares for the body and 2 squares for the head half the size of the body. Ears are same size as the head, but are only knitted to the halfway row, then cast off. Legs and arms are knitted like the tie bow, but for 6 rows, filled with wool and stitched lengthways. Sew up and pad the body and head as you sew. Then sew the ears on. A little doll can be made from squares the same way, but give it a squareknit dress, and a squareknit hat sewn like a button, but not gathered too tightly.

Doll's Clothes: Take any pattern and knit it in miniature.

Teacosy: There are many more ways to knit teacosies. They are really very simple.

Cushion: Using scraps of wool for the stripes and 100 g of wool for the main colour, knit the basic square inc, then the halfway row. Knit the basic square dec and fasten off. Make 2. Sew 3 side seams, and sew up the last seam. Add tassels to the corners.

Potholders: Knit 2 basic squares the size required, and put a piece of old towelling between the layers to make the potholder thicker before you sew up the seams.

Dishcloths: Knit a basic square the size you want in unbleached cotton. These are great on stalls, and very quick to knit, but use the cheapest cotton you can find.

Tidy-all: This uses 50 g 8-ply wool in the main colour, 50 g 8-ply wool in a contrast colour, and 1 curtain ring.
Using the main colour knit the basic pattern to 40 sts.
Knit the halfway row, then knit the basic square dec to 14 sts.
On these 14 sts start the basic square inc again to 40 sts.
Knit the halfway row, then the basic dec to 14 sts.
Once again knit from these 14 sts the basic inc to 40 sts.
Knit the halfway row, and then the basic dec down to 6 sts.
Cast off.
To knit the pockets, knit the basic square inc to 35 sts. Knit the halfway row, and then the basic dec down to 25 sts. Cast off. Make 3.
Sew the pockets on evenly, then sew a curtain ring to the top 6 sts.
If you want to decorate the pockets, do so before you sew them on.

Flowers: Flowers can be knitted any size, and look great in unpicked, unwashed 3 or 4-ply wool, also in a fine bouclé . Knit following the Poppy pattern on page 37. Sew the petals all together at the base and attach them firmly to a wire

stem. This isn't always as easy as it sounds, but you'll get there. Add some florist's stamens.

TOILET BAG

Materials   *Illustrated on page 62*
variety of knitting cotton (approx. 100 g)
5 mm needles

Back

Knitting the basic pattern, inc from 2 sts to 64 sts.
Knit the halfway row.
Then knit the basic dec until you have 46 sts left.
Now knit a row of eyelets for the cord, *k2, m1, k2 tog* along the row.
Knit 2 rows without any shaping, then cast off.

Front

Knit the basic square inc as for the back. When you get to 16 sts you might like to knit a few rows in a lacy pattern. This is very easy—knit the inc, then *k1, m1, k2 tog* along the row. It does not matter if the sts do not keep in sequence. (It is easier to leave 4 sts plain at the end than to pattern them.)
Continue knitting stripes with gt st until you have 64 sts on the needle.

Finish the front as for the back, then sew up the side seams. If you can crochet make yourself a cord, if not, twist some of the cotton you have over to make one.

It is not necessary to line the bag, but a good idea is to use part of an old pillow-case. As I do not like sewing with a machine I will always look for a simple way out; since the pillow-case seams are already sewn, you only have to cut to size, then turn the top in and stitch it to the bag.

To prevent stretching, make the lining slightly smaller than the outer bag. Sometimes by the time we have put everything in the bag but the kitchen sink, it has become twice as large as it was. As I am a very bad offender, I always make the lining about 6 cm smaller!

A tip here: if you have knitted a bag with a knitted strap, sew two buttons on, one inside, one outside, where the bag top and strap meet on each side. Older style 4-hole buttons are excellent for this type of support.

Another tip: do not make the strap too long. I am not very tall and once knitted myself a bag to match a garment. The bag looked great until I loaded it up and put it on my shoulder. What a disaster—the thing was down to my ankles! Take it from me, short straps are the answer.

Elegance, knitted in a mixture of colours and stitches
(page 60)

Martian doll (page 61)

Teacosy (page 61)

The simple toilet bag can, if you wish, become a showcase
for fancy stitches (page 63)

Guyon the Cat (page 60)

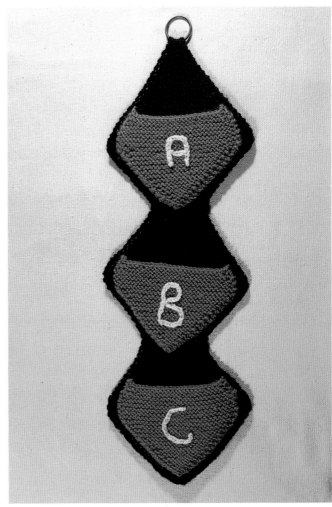

A three-pocket tidy-all (page 61)

A cheerfully striped and tasselled cushion and a stuffed ball—ways of using up small quantities of wool (page 61)

Follow the instructions from the Poppy jumper on page 37 to knit the petals for this cheerful beauty

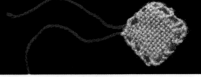

Knit a small basic square inc to 8 sts. Fasten off, leaving a long tail thread, which you sew around the square in running stitch. Pull the thread up tightly, sewing it through the middle and back again. This can be a flower centre, a button or a spot for Domino (page 33)

Index